Deaf Culture
A to Z

Walter Paul Kelley

Illustrated by Tony Landon McGregor

BuTo, Ltd. Co.  Austin, Texas

Deaf Culture A to Z

Inquiries should be addressed to
BuTo, Ltd, Co.
P.O. Box 9018
Austin, Texas 78766-9018 USA
www.buto.biz

First Printing (May 2003)
10 9 8 7 6 5 4 3 2

Library of Congress Cataloging-in-Publication Data
Kelley, Walter Paul
Deaf Culture A to Z/Walter Paul Kelley;
illustrated by Tony Landon McGregor
      p. cm.
Summary: An alphabetic look at Deaf culture.
ISBN 0-9729569-0-5 Hdk
1. Deaf - Social life and customs - Juvenile literature
2. Culture - Deaf - Juvenile literature
[1. Deaf 2. Culture 3. Alphabet]
I. McGregor, Tony Landon, ill. II. Title
HV 2392.K4552003
362.42 - dc22
LC 2003093189

Printed in the United States of America

For all children to enjoy and learn about Deaf culture

Words from the Author

In this book, you will see the word "Deaf" (with a capital D). People belonging to the Deaf community prefer to use this spelling. Deaf people identify closely with each other. They share a sense of Deaf pride, traditions, values, lifestyles, humor, folklore, art, theater, as well as a rich common language – American Sign Language. The purpose of this book is to teach all about the culture Deaf people cherish. WPK

A is for American Sign Language. American Sign Language (ASL) is the language of signs used among many Deaf people. Each sign represents a word or words. In the picture on the right, the boy is signing, "What should I do?" The librarian answers, "You can read a book on Deaf Culture." ASL is a beautiful language and it is fun to learn.

B is for Bed Vibrator. The bed vibrator is a small device used to wake up Deaf people. The device is placed under a bed mattress or under a pillow. A cord connects the device to a clock. When the clock rings, the device begins to vibrate. In the picture, the boy is reaching for the clock to turn off the vibrator. It is time for him to get up and get ready for school.

C is for Captions. Captions are words placed at the top or bottom of a movie or television screen. The captions help people see what is being said. They can be either open- or closed-captioned. Movies are usually open-captioned and television programs are usually close-captioned. Closed-captions can be easily turned on or off while open-captions cannot.

D is for "DeVIA." DeVIA is the name given to Deaf art. DeVIA means Deaf View/Image Art. There are several well-known Deaf artists who paint Deaf-related themes. One well-known artist is Dr. Betty Miller, who is in the picture on the left. Dr. Miller is considered the mother of DeVIA. She invented the idea for the art movement that expresses Deaf feelings and views.

E is for E-mail. E-mail (electronic mail) is the exchange of messages through the use of a computer or pager. Today, many Deaf people use e-mail to communicate with each other. The lady in the picture is sending a message to her boyfriend. She is thanking him for letting her know that he will be late for dinner.

F is for Fingerspelling. Deaf people spell out the letters of the alphabet with their fingers. For example, the letter "A" is made with a closed fist with the thumb on the outside. Fingerspelling is used mostly for names of people and places. It is also used to specify brand names found on food labels and other things. It can be used along with ASL. In the picture, the children are fingerspelling the word "love" that the teacher aide is signing. Fingerspelling helps Deaf children learn to spell.

G is for Gestures. Gestures are made with facial, hand, and body movements. They are used to show thoughts and feelings. Deaf people use gestures along with signs while communicating with others. Deaf actors often use many gestures while sharing stories, poetry, and prose. Look at the picture. What do you think the two Deaf actors are doing?

H is for Hearing Ear Dog. A hearing ear dog is used to alert Deaf people to sounds. The dog in the picture is responding to a doorbell. Afterwards, the dog will go to the Deaf person to let him know that someone is at the door. Other sounds the dog will respond to are baby cries, smoke alarms, phone rings, and suspicious sounds inside or outside the house. Hearing ear dogs are well cared for and much loved by those who own them.

I is for Interpreter. An interpreter is a person who signs to Deaf people what is being said. The interpreter also voices what the Deaf person is signing. Interpreters are found in many places such as schools, courtrooms, and hospitals. In the picture, Daniel, an interpreter, is signing "basketball." Daniel interprets for the Deaf players at all of the school's basketball games.

J is for Dr. I. King Jordan. Dr. Jordan was the first Deaf president of Gallaudet University. He became president in 1988, after the famous "Deaf President Now" march. Many students attending Gallaudet marched for a Deaf president because the president at that time was a hearing person who could not sign. The students wanted a person who could communicate easily with them.

K is for "KODA," kids of Deaf adults. Kodas can be either Deaf or hearing. Kodas usually grow up in the Deaf world. They learn ASL as their first language and learn the ways of Deaf people. Many hearing kodas learn English as a second language and become interpreters when they are adults. In the picture, the Deaf father is telling his son that the ocean waters are cold.

L is for Light Flasher. Light flashers are used to alert Deaf people. Light flashers help let parents know that their baby needs attention and alert individuals that their phone is ringing. They also warn families that there's smoke in the house. In the picture, the baby is making sounds to make the lamp flash for his parents to come to his crib.

M is for Museum. Many schools for the Deaf have museums. These museums are places where many people go to learn about the past. Some old things the museums keep are books, clothes, and furniture. Often, former students donate things to the museums. Visitors to the museums like to learn how Deaf children were taught and what was used in the schools to teach the children.

N is for Name Signs. Many Deaf people have name signs. Name signs are usually signed somewhere near or on the upper part of the body. In the picture, the boy on the left is asking the other boy for his name. The other boy says his name is "William" with the letter "W" placed in front of his chest. Do you have a sign name? If not, ask a Deaf person to help you to create one.

O is for Organization. An organization is a group of people working together. In many organizations for the Deaf, people meet to have fun, to discuss new and old laws, or to share ideas. Organizations can be either big or small state, national, or world gatherings. One well-known organization mainly for Deaf teenagers is the Junior National Association of the Deaf (JrNAD).

P is for "PAH." "Pah" is a signed word meaning "finally," or "at last." This word is thought to have started during the "Deaf President Now" march in 1988. In the picture, the young lady is signing "pah" because her cross-country bicycle team has just finished traveling from San Francisco to Washington, DC. She is thrilled that her team has finally completed the long and tiring cycling trip.

Q is for Quotation. A quotation is a phrase or passage that people say for others to remember. One notable quotation is "Deaf people can do anything except hear." In the picture on the right, the two teenagers are proud to say that they can be anything they wish even though they are not able to hear.

R is for Residential School. Many Deaf children attend residential schools that have classes as well as places where they can eat, sleep, and play. Residential schools are usually found in or near state capitals. Deaf Culture is reported to have begun in residential schools where the students and teachers sign to each other. Is there a residential school for the Deaf in your state?

S is for Storytelling. Deaf people love to share stories. Sometimes the stories are funny while others are quite serious. Many Deaf people love to tell what happened in the past. In the picture, a Deaf medicine man is telling the children his story of growing up in the American Indian, the Deaf, and the hearing worlds. The children are fascinated with what the medicine man has to say.

T is for Teletype device or teletext device. These devices are used to help Deaf people communicate through the phone line. Instead of speaking, Deaf people type in what they want to say. In the picture, the girl is reading what her mother on the other side of the line is typing. The mother is saying that she is happy that her daughter had a smooth flight.

U is for University. One well-known university for the Deaf is Gallaudet University. Gallaudet University was the first one established for Deaf students who completed high school. The university was named after Thomas Gallaudet, who founded it in 1865. It is located in Washington, D.C., the nation's capital. In the picture on the right, the guide is showing the girl how to sign "Gallaudet."

V is for Video Relay Services.
Video Relay Services allows Deaf
people to contact a video relay
interpreter via a web cam through
their own computer. The interpreter
then translates the Deaf caller's ASL
into speech for hearing users and
speech into ASL for Deaf users.
In the picture, the boy is telling his
friend about his trip to the Olympics
for the Deaf through the interpreter.

W is for Waving Applause. Instead of clapping, Deaf people twist their arms and hands above their heads. The hand wave is often used after a person has spoken or when something good has happened. In the picture on the right, the children are waving their hands because their school was chosen as a Blue Ribbon school. Students in the school had performed well on their tests in reading and mathematics.

X is for xylophone, a musical instrument. Many small Deaf children are trained to listen and identify different sounds made by the instrument. In the picture on the left, the young Deaf child is listening for sounds her teacher is making. The teacher will be able to identify what the child can and cannot hear.

Y is for Youth Camp. Many Deaf children attend youth camps to have fun, to learn how to play different sports, and to develop leadership skills. There are many activities in youth camps for all to enjoy. Youth camps for Deaf children can be found in almost every state. Is there one near you?

Z is for Dr. Elizabeth Zinser. Dr. Zinser was president of Gallaudet University for a very short time. Many Deaf people marched against Dr. Zinser because she could hear and could not sign. Deaf children also joined the 1988 "Deaf President Now" march asking for a Deaf president. After a few days, Dr. Zinser resigned to allow a Deaf person to be president of the university. Many Deaf people remember this major historical event.

Walter Paul Kelley, a long-time educator of Deaf/Hard of Hearing children, received his Ph.D. in the area of multicultural special education at the University of Texas at Austin. He received his B.A. degree at Baylor University in Waco, Texas, and his M.A. degree at Gallaudet University in Washington, D.C. Dr. Kelley, one of the founders of the Intertribal Deaf Council (IDC), is on its Council of Elders and has spoken on the American Indian Deaf/Hard of Hearing at different national conferences and conventions. He also presented papers on the need of more children's picture books on Deaf culture and history. Dr. Kelley is a member of the Society of Children's Book Writers and Illustrators, the Texas Writers Association, the American Library Association, and Deaf History Internatianal (DHI) and is a partner of Friends of Libraries for Deaf Action (FOLDA). Victory Week, a children's picture book on the 1988 Deaf President Now (DPN) March in Washington, DC, published in 2001 by Deaf Life Press, was his first book. Deaf Culture A to Z is his second book.

Tony Landon McGregor received his B.A., B.F.A., and M.Ed. degrees at the University of Texas at Austin (UT-Austin). He received his Ph.D. in multicultural special education also at UT-Austin. For several years, he worked as a resident artist-in-education at the Austin Museum of Art in Austin, Texas. Dr. McGregor, usually called "Tony Mac," is a nationally well known Deaf artist and his works have been featured at several state, national, and international shows such as the Texas State Arts and Crafts Show, Kentucky DeaFestival, Texas Crafts Exhibition at Winedale, "Spotlight on Deaf Artists II," "Elements of Deaf Culture," "Seeing through Deaf Eyes," and Deaf Way II. Additional information on Tony Mac can be found in Deaf Artists in America: Colonial to Contemporary, written by Dr. Debbie M. Sonnenstrahl. Tony Mac also rendered the illustrations in Victory Week.